For Anne

Methuen/Moonlight
First published 1983 by Editions Gallimard
First published 1985 in Great Britain by Methuen
Children's Books Ltd, 11 New Fetter Lane, London EC4
in association with Moonlight Publishing Ltd,
131 Kensington Church Street, London W8
Illustrations © 1983 by Editions Gallimard
English text and selection of poems © 1985
by Moonlight Publishing Ltd

Printed in Italy by La Editoriale Libraria

ISBN 0907144535

SPRING

DISCOVERERS

by Laurence Ottenheimer
adapted and edited by Alex Campbell

illustrations by Georges Lemoine

methuen ● moonlight

The year's at the spring
And day's at the morn;
Morning's at seven;
The hill-side's dew-pearl'd;
The lark's on the wing;
The snail's on the thorn;
God's in His heaven —
All's right with the world!

Robert Browning

This book belongs to

. . . .

Spring is like a perhaps hand
(which comes carefully
out of Nowhere) arranging
a window, into which people look (while
people stare
arranging and changing placing
carefully there a strange
thing and a known thing here) and

changing everything carefully

e.e. cummings

March

21	First day of spring St Benedict
22	
23	
24	
25	Annunciation and Lady Day

Spring begins at the spring equinox, on or around 21 March. At the equinox, day and night are of equal length.

26	
27	
28	*March borrowit from April three days and they were ill:*
29	*The first was frost, The second snow,*
30	*The third as cauld as it could blow.*
31	Scottish saying

Listen, buds,
it's March
twenty-first;
Don't you know
enough to
burst?

What though the
blasts of Winter
sting?

Officially,
at least,
it's Spring.

Ogden Nash

An oak tree on the first day of April
Is as bare as the same oak in December
But it looks completely different.

Now it bristles, it is a giant brazier
Of invisible glare, an invisible sun.

Ted Hughes

April

At the beginning of April, sunrise is at about 6.30 am and sunset about 7.35 pm. Every day this month, the sun rises about 2 minutes earlier and sets about 1½ minutes later.

1st April

The first of April, some do say,
Is set apart for All Fools' Day,
But why people call it so,
Nor I nor they themselves
*   do know.*

It is an old custom to play practical jokes on 1 April, traditionally before the stroke of noon. People are sent on fools' errands: to buy bull's milk or striped paint, for instance. They may be given salt in the sugar bowl or plastic fried eggs for breakfast. Anyone taken in by these tricks is called an April Fool. In Scotland the fooled person is called an *April Gowk*, which means 'cuckoo', in Yorkshire an *April Noddy*; and in France an *April Fish*.

*So here we are in April,
in showy, blowy April,
In frowsy, blowsy April,
the rowdy, dowdy time;*

2

3

4

If by April 3 there's
    no cuckoo,
His wife is ill,
    and the year is too.

5

6

*April weather,
Rain and
    sunshine,
Both together.*

7

8

In England there is always
great excitement over hearing
the first cuckoo of spring, with
letters to the papers about it.

9

10

11

12

April snow stays no longer
than water on a trout's back.

13

14

In soppy, sloppy April,
in wheezy, breezy April,
In ringing, stinging April,
with a singing swinging rhyme.

Ted
Robinson

15

16

17
18 As the weather grows
warmer, buds begin to open
and young birds are born.
Watch out for their nests in
trees and hedgerows.

19

20

April, April,
Laugh thy golden
laughter;
But the moment
after,
Weep thy golden
tears!
William Watson

21

22

23 Feast of St George,
patron saint of England

24

25 *When April*
blows his horn,

26 *It's good for*
hay and corn.

27

April brings the primrose sweet,
Scatters daisies at our feet.

Sara Coleridge

28

29
Till April's dead,
Change not a thread.

30

Palm Sunday

The Sunday before Easter is the feast of Christ's triumphant entry into Jerusalem. As he came to the city, riding on a donkey, rejoicing crowds greeted him with branches of palm.

In commemoration of this day, pieces of palm are given out in Christian churches. People put them up in their homes till the following year.

Nowadays palm is imported from hot countries, such as Spain. But in the old days, people went out into the woods on Palm Saturday to pick greenery, especially branches of willow which is sometimes called 'English palm'.

Afield for palms the girls repair,
And sure enough the palms are there,
And each will find by hedge or pond
Her waving silver-tufted wand.

A.E. Housman

Easter

Easter is the feast of Christ's resurrection. Early Christians believed that on this day the sun danced in the sky for joy that Christ was risen from the dead.

In Britain on the days leading up to Easter, and especially on Good Friday, we eat *hot-cross buns*: spiced buns decorated with a cross. This custom is even older than Christianity; the Romans used to eat bread marked with a cross in honour of Diana, the moon goddess. Some people think that the cross originally represented the quarters of the moon. Now, of course, it reminds us that Christ died on the cross.

Easter was, and still is, a time of tremendous rejoicing, coming at the end of the forty lean days of Lent. It is celebrated on the Sunday after the first full moon following the spring equinox. This means Easter may fall any time between 22 March and 25 April.

April moon The moon in the month that follows Easter is often accompanied by frosts and icy winds that can kill or damage young plants.

Spring bursts today
For Christ is risen and all
The earth's at play.

Christina Rossetti

Easter eggs

I want an egg for Easter,
A browny egg for Easter,
I want an egg for Easter,
So I'll tell my brown hen.

I'll take her corn
and water,
And show her what I've brought her,
And she'll lay my egg for Easter,
Inside her little pen.

Irene F. Pawsey

Tip-top tip-top
tap a speckled egg.
Once to put him in his cup
and twice to crack his head.

Michael Rosen

Egg Sunday was a name for Easter in the Middle Ages. The egg is a symbol of new life. People used to play games with them. Children used to ask for *pace-eggs* ('pace' comes from *paschalis*, the old Latin word for Easter), and would run with them balanced on a spoon, or roll them downhill, to see which would go furthest. The eggs were hard-boiled, of course . . .

Easter eggs now are usually made of chocolate or sugar. But in earlier times people gave each other decorated hens' eggs. You can dye eggs yourself with cake colouring, or using vegetables.

Boil the eggs in water with onion skins to turn them orange, or spinach to turn them green.

*All in this pleasant evening, together come are we
For the summer springs so fresh, green and gay;
We tell you of a blossoming and buds on every tree,
Drawing near unto the merry month of May.*

*Rise up, the children of this house, all in your rich attire,
For the summer springs so fresh, green and gay;
And every hair upon your heads shines like silver wire
Drawing near unto the merry month of May.*

Anon.

May

At the beginning of May, sunrise is about 5.35 am and sunset about 8.25 pm. The sun rises about 1½ minutes earlier and sets about 1½ minutes later than the day before.

1 May Day

Before dawn on 1 May, people used to go out into the woods and fields to gather flowers. They put up a maypole, a tall pole decorated with flowers, and danced around it. This tradition, the celebration of love and rebirth, dates back to the Romans, and beyond.

To the May-pole haste away For it is a holiday.

Anon.

The figure of May opposite is holding a picture of Venus which is part of a larger painting, *The Birth of Venus*, by Botticelli, a fifteenth-century Italian painter. Venus was the Roman goddess of beauty and love.

Nowadays 1 May is Labour Day, the holiday dedicated to workers.

With Hal-an-Tow! Jolly Rumble, O!
For we are up as soon as any day, O,
And for to fetch the summer home,
The Summer and the May, O.

Anon.

March winds and April showers
Bring forth May flowers.

Anon.

2 Trust not a day ere birth of May.

3

4
5
I love my little brother
and sister every day
But I seem to love them best
in the merry month of May.

Anon.

6

7
8
Who doffs his coat on a winter's day
Will gladly put it on in May.

9

10

Who shears his sheep before St Servatius' Day loves more his wool than his sheep.

11 St Mamertus

12 St Pancras

13 St Servatius

Saints Mamertus, Pancras and Servatius are known as the saints of ice in Europe, because their feast days are usually frosty.

18

May brings flocks of pretty lambs
Skipping by their fleecy dams.

Sara Coleridge

14

15 He who bathes in May
Will soon be laid in clay.

16

17

18

19 From your apple trees keep
the witches away,

20 Or they'll blight the bloom on
St Dunstan's Day.

21

22

23

24 *The flow'ry May who from*
her green lap throws

25 *The yellow Cowslip and the*
pale Primrose.

John Milton

26

A swarm of bees
in May
Is worth a load of
hay;
A swarm of bees
in June
Is worth a silver
spoon;
A swarm of bees
in July
Is not worth a fly.

Anon.

*The palm and may
make country hours gay.
Lambs frisk and play,
the shepherds pipe all day.*   Thomas Nashe

27
28

Mist in May, heat in June,
Make the harvest come right soon.

29

30

31

Cast not a clout,
Till May be out.

*Lady-bird,
lady-bird!
fly away home!
The field-mouse
has gone to her nest,
The daisies have
shut up their
sleepy red eyes,
And the bees and
the birds are at
rest.*

Caroline Southey

*As I was a-walking
One morning in spring,
I heard a pretty ploughboy,
So sweetly he did sing;
And as he was a-singing
These words I heard him say:
'Oh, there's no life like the
ploughboy
All in the month of May.'*

*There's the lark in the morning,
She will rise up from her nest,
She'll mount the white air
With the dew on her breast,
And with the pretty ploughboy O,
She'll whistle and she'll sing,
And at night she'll return
To her nest back again.*

Anon.

May Feasts

Ascension Day
Forty days after Easter, Christians celebrate the Ascension, the day on which Christ was taken up into Heaven.

Whit Sunday
Fifty days after Easter is the feast of Whitsun, or *Pentecost*. The Bible tells that on this day the Holy Spirit, which is often pictured as a dove, came down to the Apostles and gave them the *gift of tongues* — they found that they could speak in many languages, to tell all peoples about Jesus.

It is the day of all the year,
Of all the year the one day,
And here I come, my Mother dear,
To bring you cheer,
A-mothering on Sunday.

Anon.

Mothering Sunday
Many countries have a special day dedicated to mothers. In Britain, it is the fourth Sunday in Lent. On this day, sons and daughters who were away from home used to visit their mothers, bringing presents of flowers or, traditionally, simnel cake. This is a special kind of fruit cake, iced with marzipan.

Spring, the sweet Spring, is the year's pleasant king;
Then blooms each thing, then maids dance in a ring,
Cold doth not sting, the pretty birds do sing,
Cuckoo, jug-jug, pu-we, to-witta-woo!

The fields breathe sweet, the daisies kiss our feet,
Young lovers meet, old wives a-sunning sit,
In every street these tunes our ears do greet,
Cuckoo, jug-jug, pu-we, to-witta-woo!
Spring! the sweet Spring!

Thomas Nashe

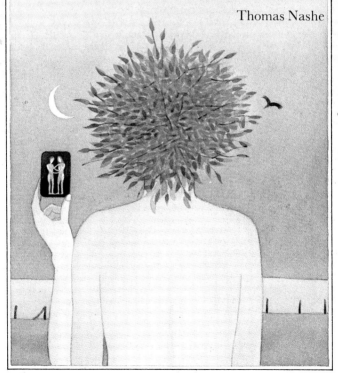

June

At the beginning of June, sunrise is at about 4.45 am and sunset at about 9.20 pm. Each day, the sun rises less than a minute earlier and sets less than a minute later than the day before, until the *summer solstice*, the longest day of the year. This falls on about 21 June.

1 Calm weather in June
Corn sets in tune.

2

3 June got its name from the
4 Roman goddess Juno,
goddess of marriage
and childbearing.

5

6

7

8 Rain on 8 June is said to mean
the summer will be wet.

9

10

*June damp and warm
Does the farmer no harm.*

11 On St Barnabas
Put the scythe to the grass.

12

13

14
15 In the United Kingdom, the monarch's official birthday falls on the second Saturday in June.

16

17

18

19
20 **Father's Day** is on the third Sunday in June in the UK, USA and Canada.

21 Summer solstice

The summer solstice is the longest day of the year, although Midsummer Day is celebrated on 24 June.

Dance for
your daddy,
My bonny
laddy,
Dance for
your daddy,
My bonny
lamb.

Anon.

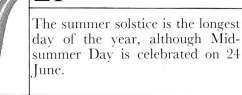

A hot day

Cottonwool clouds loiter.
A lawnmower, very far,
Birrs. Then a bee comes
To a crimson rose and softly
Deftly and fatly crams
A velvet body in.

A tree, June-lazy, makes
A tent of dim green light.
Sunlight weaves in the leaves,
Honey-light laced with leaf-light,
green interleaved with gold.
Sunlight gathers its rays
In sheaves, which the wind unweaves
And then reweaves.

A.S.J. Tessimond

The sky in spring

Here are the stars as they appear in
the month of June.

Looking north

1 The Charioteer   2 Cassiopeia   3 Cepheus   4 Vega
5 The Little Bear   6 The Dragon   7 The Great Bear
8 The Lion

A clear night in spring is a good time to observe the stars. Use these star maps to help you to identify some of the major constellations.

Looking south

1 The Scorpion   2 The Scales   3 Virgo   4 The Crow
5 Hydra   6 The Great Bear   7 The Wagoner
8 Hercules

Hailstones and rainbows

A sunshiny shower Won't last an hour.

In spring we never know what the weather will do next. All the proverbs warn us that, however bright it seems, it is safest to stay warmly dressed: 'Till April's dead, change not a thread', or 'Cast not a clout (any clothing), till May be out'.

One moment the sun shines, the next it showers with rain. Hail may fall suddenly. The swirling currents of air caused by the warming sun and the still-cold ground causes water-vapour (rain) and sometimes ice particles (hail) to be swept down from the clouds towards the earth. But the showers are usually over as suddenly as they begin.

My heart leaps up when I behold
A rainbow in the sky;
So was it when my life began,
So is it now I am a man.

William Wordsworth

Often in spring, sun and showers appear at the same time, giving us rainbows.

A rainbow forms when the sun shines on the millions of raindrops in the sky. As they pass through the raindrops, the sun's rays break up into the separate colours which make up the sun's white light: red, orange, yellow, green, blue, indigo, violet.

A rainbow always appears reflected in the sky opposite to the sun.

Legend has it that there is treasure buried at the end of a rainbow. Unfortunately, as a rainbow is only made of light-waves, the end moves as you do, so it's impossible to find out if the legend is true.

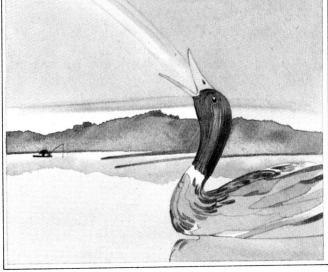

Clouds

*There's joy
in the
mountains:
Small clouds
are sailing,
Blue sky is
prevailing:
The rain
is over
and gone.*

William
Wordsworth

Rain comes from clouds, which are made of water. Even the smallest cloud we see in the sky is carrying between 100 and 1,000 tons of water in the form of tiny drops.

The water in the atmosphere goes round and round. The heat of the sun draws up tiny drops from ponds, rivers, seas: this is called *evaporation*. But as the clouds rise in the sky and get cooler, the water droplets become too heavy for the air to hold; they fall as rain.

Cirrus
Wispy white clouds which are often a sign of bad weather.

Cirro-stratus
A thin veil of cloud; when it covers the sun or moon they seem to have a halo of light around them.

Alto-stratus
Fine clouds, often accompanied by rain.

Nimbo-stratus
Thick, dark grey clouds, bringing rain or snow.

Alto-cumulus
'Mackerel sky': patchy clouds in lines, a sign of bad weather.

Cumulo-nimbus
Great thick clouds shaped like mountains or towers, often bringing stormy weather.

Strato-cumulus
Big low grey clouds, sometimes bringing rain.

Stratus
Uniform low grey clouds, like a layer of fog.

Cumulus
Thick fluffy white clouds in a blue sky.

The budding leaves

For the sun
Is shining fair,
And the green
Is on the tree;
And the wind
Is everywhere
Whispering,
So urgently.

James Stephens

As the days grow warmer and longer, the roots of trees start to draw water from the soil. Sap, which is water mixed with food, rises up the tree, to feed the buds which for nine months have rested on the branch, protected from cold weather by their outer scales, waiting for the spring.

The buds swell. The tiny, tightly furled leaves inside them unfold, forcing open their outer scales. A new shoot emerges and grows towards the sunlight. Some buds produce leaves and a twig; others, a flower.

When blackthorn petals pearl
the breeze,
There are the twisted hawthorn
trees
Thick-set with buds, as clear
and pale
As golden water or green hail.

Mary Webb

*The spring comes linking and jinking
through the woods,
Opening wi' gentle hand the bonnie green
and yellow buds.*

William Miller

Birds feed on buds, especially in the spring. As the tree is preparing to come into leaf, the buds fill with a rich substance that is very nourishing to birds.

*The trees are
coming into leaf
Like something
almost being
said.*

Philip Larkin

Chestnut

Beech

Ash

Hornbeam

Poplar

Walnut

Cherry

Rowan

Elm

Trees in blossom

The flowers that blossom on a tree in spring produce fruit and seed later in the year. Pages 80 and 81 show how the flower of the cherry tree develops into the cherry we eat.

A flower can only produce seed after it has been fertilized. This happens when *pollen*, a yellow powder from the male part of a flower, reaches the little eggs, called *ovules*, in the female part.

Let there be Light!
In pink and white
The apple tree
blooms for our
delight.

Oliver St John
Gogarty

On fruit trees, such as the cherry, every flower has both male and female parts, and produces both pollen and ovules. Other species, such as the oak, have separate male and female flowers growing on the same tree. In still other species, such as the poplar and the willow, male and female flowers grow on different trees. All trees bear flowers, to make the seed from which new trees can grow.

Loveliest of trees, the cherry now
Is hung with bloom along the bough,
And stands about the woodland ride
Wearing white for Eastertide.

A.E. Housman

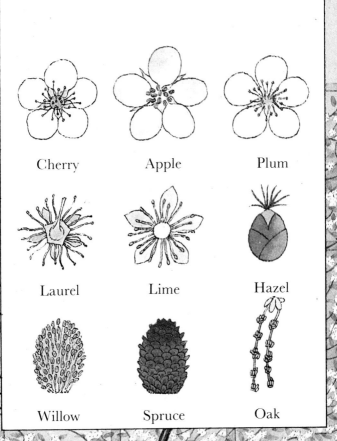

Cherry　　　　Apple　　　　Plum

Laurel　　　　Lime　　　　Hazel

Willow　　　　Spruce　　　　Oak

The blackbird
and the earthworm

*Strange beautiful
unquiet thing,
Lone flute of
God, how can
you sing
Winter to spring?*

Joseph Auslander

The blackbird

At dawn and in the evening during spring, we hear the song of the blackbird. Before the leaves are out, he is easily seen singing from the bare branches of a tree. The male blackbird is black, with an orange beak. The female is brown, with a brown beak.

The blackbird eats insects, earthworms, fruit and seeds. It feeds on the ground, and bends its head to left and right at each step as it looks for food, because its eyes are on the sides on its head.

When it spots a worm, the blackbird pulls it from the earth with its beak . . . and swallows it.

Earthworms

Worms do not like light or heat, and only come out at night. They breathe through their skins, which have to be kept moist.

Worms are very useful to the gardener. The tunnels they dig underground allow water and air to enter the soil and so help plants to grow. The worm's droppings, called *wormcasts*, also help to feed plants.

A bird came down the walk:
He did not know I saw;
He bit an angle-worm in halves
And ate the fellow, raw.

Emily Dickinson

Songbirds

Spring is the time when birds choose their mates, build their nests, lay their eggs and rear their young. And spring is the time of birdsong. Early in the season, male birds sing to attract a mate. When a male has found a site for his nest, he sings almost continually to let other birds know that this is his territory.

With every sweet apostle
That spreads the news of spring,
Linnet and lark and throstle,
Blackcap and redwing,
I too begin to sing.

Andrew Young

The saddest noise, the sweetest noise,
The maddest noise that grows,
The birds, they make it in the spring,
At night's delicious close

Between the March and April line,
That magical frontier
Beyond which summer hesitates,
Almost too heavenly near.

Emily Dickinson

Wood-pigeon
'coooo-co'

Magpie
'chak-chak'

Quail
'quic-ic-ic'

Nightingale
'chook-chook
piu, piu, piu'

Crow
'caw, caw, caw'

Skylark
'chirr-r-up'

Blue tit
'tsee-tsit'

Jay
'skraaak'

Sparrow
'cheep, cheep'

Courtship and mating

Do you ask what the birds say? The Sparrow, the Dove,
The Linnet and Thrush say, 'I love and I love!'
In the winter they're silent — the wind is so strong;
What it says, I don't know, but it sings a loud song.
But green leaves, and blossoms, and sunny warm weather,
And singing, and loving — all come back together.

Samuel Taylor Coleridge

The birds around me hopped and played,
Their thoughts I cannot measure:
But the least motion which they made,
It seems a thrill of pleasure. William Wordsworth

The courtship of birds in spring is fascinating to watch. Usually the male puts on a special show to win the female.

Some sing their finest songs. Others, such as the finch, which do not have such good voices, spread out their wings to show their handsome feathers, or fly about spectacularly.

The redstart, in the picture opposite, utters a high-pitched hissing note as he displays his wings to his chosen mate.

The wagtail displays his yellow belly.

The male sparrow performs a little dance, dropping his wings, ruffling the feathers on his head and bowing to the female.

When birds have chosen their mates, they build a nest where the female will lay her eggs.

Pleasure it is
To hear, iwis,
The birdës sing,
The deer in the
dale,
The sheep in the
vale,
The corn
springing.

William Cornish

Nest building

Some nests are built like open baskets, others like proper little houses with roof and entrance. Every kind of bird has its particular style of nest and chooses a particular kind of site.

The great tit and the blue tit build their nests in holes in trees and walls; the hedge-sparrow and nightingale low down in hedgerows; rooks and crows in the tops of trees; the swallow and house-sparrow under the roof; the blackbird in low trees or bushes; and the skylark nests on the ground in a field.

Materials for birds' nests are wonderfully varied: twigs and mud, leaves, wool, moss, feathers — even spiders' webs.

Reed warbler
nest of woven grass

Long-tailed tit
nest of moss
and grass

**Hedge sparrow
or dunnock**
moss nest

Skylark
grass nest

Goldcrest
nest of moss
and cobwebs

Swallow
nest of mud and
dry grass

Bird's eggs

*As I was walking
in a field of
wheat,
I picked up
something
good to eat;
Neither fish, flesh,
fowl nor bone,
I kept it till
it ran alone.*

Answer:

An egg

Birds sit on their eggs to keep them warm. They turn them regularly, to make sure that every part of each egg is kept at the same temperature. If eggs get too cold they will not hatch.

Some parent birds take turns sitting, but in the case of the blackbird only the female sits. The male brings her food and drives away anyone who comes too close.

The female blackbird, like the female of many bird species, has duller colouring than the male. This makes her hard to see, so that enemies are less likely to notice her sitting in her nest.

Eggs too are protected from animals and birds who might eat them, by the colouring of their shells. Plovers and other birds which nest on open ground lay speckled, dull eggs which look much the same as the earth around them.

Tit

Cuckoo

Swallow

Quail

Skylark

Sparrow

Thrush

Wren

Turtle-dove

Magpie

Crow

Jay

45

Nestlings

Baby birds are helpless when they first hatch; they cannot fly, nor feed themselves. Their parents fly to and from the nest from morning till night, gathering food and bringing it back to their hungry children. The coal tit feeds its young 350 times a day.

As soon as the nestlings spot one of their parents returning, they stretch out their necks and open wide their beaks, ready to swallow an insect.

They grow quickly. A young robin weighs only two grams when it hatches, but twelve days later it weighs ten times as much!

Garden warbler

With bill and breasts
They build their nests,
Then lay and hatch their young;
They feed them too,
All this they do,
And spare some time for song.

William Ronksley

47

The first flowers

The first flowers of the spring bloom early, before leaves are on the trees. In woodlands and along the hedgerows we find primroses, violets, wood anemones and daffodils, while bluebells carpet the ground with a blue haze.

Only early in the year do the woodland flowers receive the sunlight they need to grow. In late spring, when the trees are fully in leaf, the ground underneath them is in shadow, and only at the wood's edges, where the sun's rays can still enter, are we likely to find many flowers.

According to legend, cowslips come from the bunch of keys St Peter uses to open the gates of Heaven.

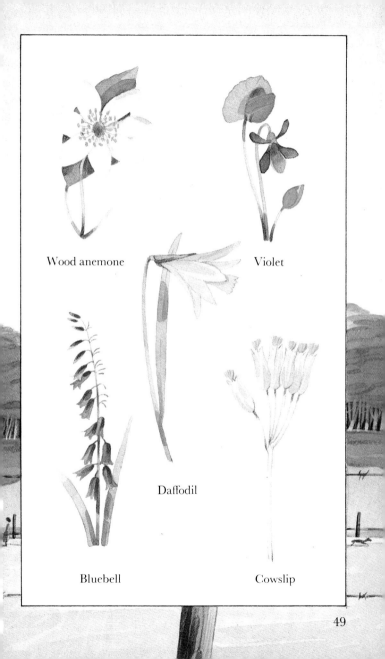

Wood anemone

Violet

Daffodil

Bluebell

Cowslip

Water plants

*All along the backwater,
Through the rushes tall,
Ducks are a-dabbling,
Up tails all!*

Kenneth Grahame

The **bulrush** or **reedmace** flowers in June. The tiny male flowers are at the top. Just below them on the same stem, are female flowers which turn into fluffy seeds.

Duckweed floats at the end of long stalks rooted in the mud below the water.

The large floating leaves of **water-lilies** are a popular resting-place for frogs.

Sagittaria is also known as **arrow-head** because of the shape of its leaves.

Water plantain

Valerian

Water iris
or yellow flag

Bulrush or reedmace

Sagittaria or
arrowhead

Duckweed

Waterlilies

From tadpole to frog

*Be kind and
   tender to the
   Frog,
And do not call
   him names,
As 'Slimy Skin' or
   'Polly-wog',
Or likewise
   'Ugly James'.*

Hilaire Belloc

In March the mother frog lays her eggs, which we call frog spawn. You can see them floating in the water in ponds, or along the edges of streams.

The eggs look like black dots, surrounded by jelly, and grouped in clusters of up to 4,000. Inside each one, a tadpole forms. After a week it wriggles out of the egg, looking more like a tiny fish than a frog. It has a long tail and no legs, and breathes like a fish through two gills at the side of its body.

Within a few days the tadpole is swimming around, feeding on tiny water plants and growing very quickly. Gradually, its gills and tail disappear, and lungs and legs develop in their place. At eight weeks it has back legs, and at eleven weeks front legs as well. By the time it is three months old, its tail has vanished completely: the tadpole is now a tiny frog.

Frog's egg

Nine days later

The tadpole grows.
It has a long tail
and external gills.

Seven weeks.
The hind legs develop.

The tail is shorter.
The forelegs have
grown.

The tail drops off.
The tadpole is now a frog.

Frogs and toads

*Five little speckled
    frogs
Sat on a speckled
    log,
Eating some most
    delicious bugs,
Yum yum.*

L. B. Scott

The frog is fully grown when it is three years old. It is *amphibious*, which means that it can live on land or in water. On land, it moves in leaps and bounds, kicking out its long hind legs. In the water, it swims with its webbed feet which act like paddles.

The frog cannot survive anywhere that is hot and dry, because it drinks and breathes through its skin, which must always be kept moist and slimy. Its greenish colour helps the frog to stay hidden among water plants or in the grass when enemies approach. Snakes, rats, hedgehogs and herons all think frogs are delicious.

The male frog has two little bags, called *vocal sacs*, at the sides of his mouth. When he croaks, the sacs blow up to the size of cherries to make his voice louder.

54

By a quiet little stream on an old mossy log,
Looking very forlorn, sat a little green frog;
He'd a sleek speckled back, and two bright yellow eyes,
And when dining, selected the choicest of flies.   Vera
Hessey

The tree frog
The young tree frog lives near lakes or ponds, until at the age of two it climbs a tree; after that, it never returns to the water except to lay eggs in the spring.

The toad
Some toads have thick, warty skins, which don't seem very beautiful. But in fact their skins protect them from attack. They produce a nasty-smelling poison which repels their enemies.

The moon is up,
The night owls
*   scritch.*
Who's that
*   croaking?*
The frog in the
*   ditch.*

James Reeves

55

Pollen's varied voyages

Garden, grow,
Quick and slow,
Some surprise
*   each morning*
*   show;*
Lovely as your
*   blue and gold,*
Are the surprises
*   you withhold.*

Eleanor Farjeon

When spring flowers first open, they are loaded with *pollen*. This yellow powder comes from the *stamens*, the male part of the flower.

The female part of the flower is called the *pistil*. It holds the ovules, which develop into seeds after pollen reaches and fertilizes them.

Some flowers are fertilized by their own pollen. This can only happen when a flower has both pistil and stamens and they ripen at the same time.

Bright colours

Many flowers are fertilized when insects or the wind carry pollen from the stamen of one flower to the pistil of another of the same species. Insects are attracted by brightly coloured and strong-smelling flowers. They fly from one to another, feeding on their nectar, and accidentally picking up and dropping pollen.

Long stamens

Flowers pollinated by the wind do not need to attract insects and are not so brightly coloured. Instead, they have long stamens and pistils which the wind can easily reach and blow the pollen off.

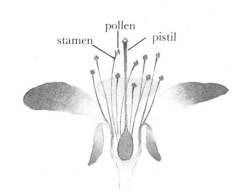

stamen pollen pistil

*Within the flower there
lies a seed,
Within the seed there
springs a tree,
Within the tree there
spreads a wood.*

Kathleen Raine

Bees

*Thousandz of
    thornz there be
On the Rozez
    where gozez
The Zebra of Zee:
Sleek, striped, and
    hairy,
The steed of the
    Fairy
Princess of Zee.*

Walter de la Mare

In a beehive there are three kinds of bee: the queen, who is the only one able to lay eggs; a few hundred males, called drones, who fertilize the eggs; and between 20,000 and 50,000 worker bees who are female, but cannot lay eggs.

All the work of the hive is done by the worker bees. They go from flower to flower collecting pollen and nectar, a sweet juice which plants produce to attract the insects that pollinate them.

The workers carry pollen packed on to their hind legs. They suck nectar through their tongues and mix it with a special saliva to make honey. Back in the hive, they regurgitate the honey into a honeycomb.

When a bee finds a good feeding-place, she does a special dance in the air just outside the hive, to show other bees how to find it.

Every worker bee has a particular job to do. Those who do not gather food work in the hive. They keep it clean and build new honeycombs. They pack pollen and nectar into the cells of the honeycombs, for the bee colony to live off in winter. Others look after the eggs, and feed the bee larvae.

Bean seed in the earth

The bean sprouts.

Roots develop, the shoot begins to show.

The shoot grows, the seed dries up.

Garden flowers

Garden flowers have different life-spans and are sown at different times of year.

Annuals, such as the petunia, nasturtium and sunflower, are sown in the spring. They grow, bloom, produce seeds and die in the same year. They have to be sown again the following spring.

Biennials, such as the foxglove, live for two years. They are sown in the summer, but do not bloom until the following spring.

Perennials, such as the peony, iris and daisy, live and bloom for many years. Though the stems die down in the autumn, the base of the plant stays alive. It stores food through the winter and produces new shoots in the spring.

The geranium and fuchsia flower every year, but only if they have been protected from frost during the winter.

Geranium

Along the blushing borders, bright with dew,
And in yon mingled wilderness of flowers,
Fair-handed Spring unbosoms every Grace:
Throws out the snow-drop, and the crocus first,
The daisy, primrose, violet darkly blue,
And polyanthus of unnumber'd dyes;
The yellow wall-flower, stain'd with iron brown;
And lavish stock that scents the garden round.

James Thomson

Fuchsia

65

Wild flowers and weeds

Dandelion salad
Pick young dandelion leaves, wash and drain them. Serve with oil-and-vinegar dressing, and sliced hard-boiled eggs.

Nettle soup
Pick 200 grams of young nettle leaves (remember to wear gloves!). Boil them in water with 4 potatoes for 20 minutes, then sieve. Return the mixture to the pan, heat, and add salt, pepper and a dash of cream just before serving.

Weeds are wild flowers that grow where the gardener or the farmer does not want them, taking food from the plants that they have sown.

But, where ground is uncultivated, weeds can grow freely. Some of them are very good to eat.

Nothing is so beautiful as spring —
When weeds, in wheels, shoot long and lovely and lush.

Gerard Manley Hopkins

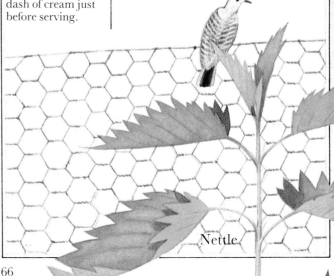

Nettle

Dandelion

Pimpernel

White clover

Thistle

A calendar of vegetables

When you hear the cuckoo shout, 'Tis time to plant your tatties out.

('Tatties' is a dialect word for potatoes.)

A lot of work has to be done in the garden in spring: preparing seeds, sowing, planting out, weeding, picking the last cabbages and leeks, putting in potatoes, carrots, onions . . .

Here is a calendar of garden work.

Sow	Plant out		Pick	
	March	**April**	**May**	**June**
Potatoes	plant	plant	plant	pick
Marrows		sow	sow	
Peas	sow	sow	sow	
Runner beans				

68

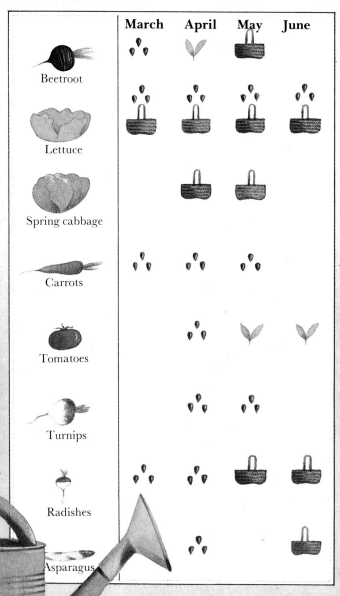

	March	April	May	June
Beetroot				
Lettuce				
Spring cabbage				
Carrots				
Tomatoes				
Turnips				
Radishes				
Asparagus				

Ants and greenfly

Ants protect themselves, and their greenfly herds, by squirting out a stinging liquid, called formic acid.

The ant has made himself illustrious
Through constant industry industrious.
So what?
Would you be calm and placid
If you were full of formic acid?

Ogden Nash

Spring is the season of birth for insects too: they invade the garden. Greenflies cluster on the stems and leaves of plants, feeding on their sap. They multiply very fast. A greenfly only lives for five days, but in a single day it can give birth to twenty other greenfly. The plant the greenflies feed on is soon starved of sap and dies, unless ladybirds come to the rescue. Ladybirds love greenfly, and can eat 100 a day!

Ants, on the other hand, herd greenfly, rather as we herd cows. They 'milk' them of honeydew, a sweet liquid which the greenfly produces and which the ants love. With its antennae, the ant strokes the greenfly's abdomen to make the honeydew come out.

Ants do not want other insects to steal their honeydew; when they find greenfly settled on low plants, they curl the leaves round to make shelters for them. In the autumn, the greenfly lay eggs which will not hatch until spring. Ants hide the eggs in a safe place, to be sure of their honeydew supply next year!

How large unto the tiny fly
Must little things appear! —
A rosebud like a feather bed,
Its prickle like a spear.

Walter de la Mare

How long does a cockchafer fly?

1 Eggs laid in the ground by the female cockchafer

2 Cockchafer larva.

3 For three years, the larva feeds on roots.

4 The larva turns into a chrysalis or pupa (August-September).

5 The cockchafer emerges in spring.

When you see a cockchafer emerging from the ground and flying towards the tree-tops, it may be the first time it has ever flown. Cockchafers spend the first three or four years of their lives underground.

The female cockchafer lays her eggs in the earth. The larva hatches from the egg, then spends the next three years underground, feeding on roots. Not until the summer of the third year does it pupate: it forms a hard case, inside which the larva transforms itself into a cockchafer and finally emerges the following spring.

Male cockchafers die at the beginning of July. Females live a few days more, just long enough to lay their eggs.

When cockchafers do emerge they feed on leaves and buds, and can do great damage to fruit trees, ruining the crop. Fortunately, though, because of the life-cycle of the cockchafer, such plagues occur only every three or four years.

1

2

3

*The insect youth are on
the wing
Eager to taste the honied
spring.*

Thomas Gray

From caterpillar to butterfly

*Was worm
swaddled in
white.
Now, tiny queen
in sequin coat
peacock-bright,
drinks the wind
and feeds
on sweat of the
leaves.
Is little chinks
of mosaic
floating,
a scatter of
coloured beads.*

May Swenson

A cabbage white butterfly. They love cabbages and can devour fields of them.

The female butterfly lays between 200 and 300 eggs in a hole in a branch. After a few days, a tiny caterpillar emerges from each egg: this is a larva.

The caterpillar feeds voraciously on leaves and greenfly, growing fast. Its skin quickly becomes too tight. The caterpillar sheds it and appears in a larger one. After three weeks of eating and several changes of skin, the caterpillar unwinds from its mouth a silk thread and weaves itself a cocoon.

Inside the cocoon, the caterpillar pupates: through the autumn and winter, it develops into a butterfly. Then, when sap rises in the trees again and buds open, the butterfly emerges from its cocoon, its wings crumpled and damp. It stretches them out in the sun to dry, and flies away.

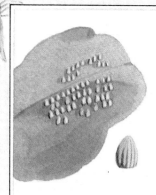

The eggs hatch.
Tiny caterpillars emerge:
the butterfly's larvae.

Butterfly eggs.

Brown and furry
Caterpillar in a hurry;
Take your walk
To the shady leaf, or stalk.

Christina Rossetti

Inside its cocoon,
the caterpillar transforms
itself into a butterfly.

Butterflies

Red Admiral caterpillar

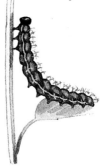

*What is a
butterfly?
At best
He's but a
caterpillar
dressed.*

We see butterflies from spring to autumn. They love the sun, and fly off to gather food as soon as it is warm enough.

The **Red Admiral** spends the winter in North Africa, and returns to our gardens for the months of May to October. It feeds on asters and fallen fruit.

The **Painted Lady** is another butterfly that migrates. It comes from the south and crosses the Mediterranean and the Alps to feed on the flowers of the thistle and nettle in May.

The **Swallowtail** is seen in meadows from June to September. Its caterpillar is a handsome green with red and orange stripes.

The **Queen of Spain Fritillary** is found in meadows between March and the autumn. Its caterpillar feeds on violet leaves and sainfoin.

Queen of
Spain Fritillary

Red Admiral

Painted Lady

Swallowtail

Moths

Most moths come out at night, and there are many more of them than there are butterflies by day. They have heavier bodies than butterflies, and their antennae are often feathery. By day moths sleep, their wings folded flat on their backs.

Privet Hawkmoth
It appears in June. Its caterpillar is found on privet hedges and lilac leaves.

Cinnabar Moth
It is found in meadows and flowery places from May to July. This moth is poisonous; its enemies recognize it by its bright colours.

Pebble Hook-tip
This moth lives in the woods. It is found near birch trees from May to July. Its caterpillar lives on aspens, poplars and birches.

Elephant Hawkmoth
It appears in gardens and flowering meadows in May and June. Its caterpillar lives on vines and honeysuckle.

Caterpillar of the Privet Hawkmoth

Privet
Hawkmoth

Cinnabar Moth

Pebble Hook-tip

Elephant Hawkmoth

From flower to fruit

The first English cherries are ripe towards the end of June, though imported ones appear in the shops earlier.

Inside the pistil of the cherry flower lies a tiny ovule. One day, an insect comes to feed on the flower, and drops some pollen on to the pistil. The pollen finds its way to the ovule and makes it fertile; now the flower can develop into a fruit.

In time, the flower withers. Its stamens and petals fall away. The ovule grows bigger and bigger and becomes a cherry-stone, hanging from the branch inside a hard green cherry.

As the weeks go by, the cherry grows sweet and juicy, and inside it the shell that protects the seed grows hard. By the end of the spring, the cherry is red and ripe for eating, and the stone holds the seed of a new tree.

Children's voices in the orchards
Between the blossom- and the fruit-time:
Golden head, crimson head,
Between the green tip and the root.

T.S. Eliot

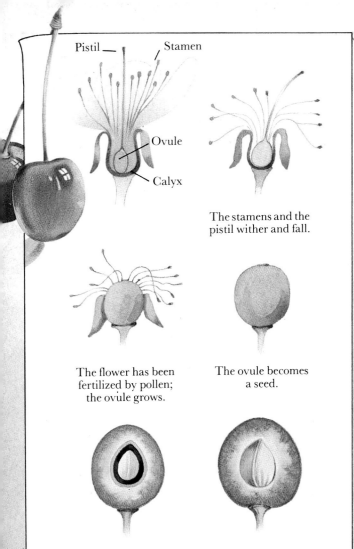

Pistil — Stamen

Ovule

Calyx

The stamens and the
pistil wither and fall.

The flower has been
fertilized by pollen;
the ovule grows.

The ovule becomes
a seed.

Fruit pulp grows
around the cherry-stone,
which is still soft.

The cherry-stone hardens:
the cherry is ripe.

Cherries and berries

Riddle me, riddle me ree,
A little man in a tree;
A stick in his hand,
A stone in his throat,
If you read me this riddle
I'll give you a groat.

Answer:
A cherry

Cherries and berries begin to appear in late spring, and continue through the summer. Cherries and strawberries come first, followed by gooseberries, red and black currants, and raspberries.

Strawberries that in gardens grow
Are plump and juicy fine,
But sweeter far, as wise men know,
Spring from the woodland vine.

No need for bowl
or silver spoon,
Sugar
or spice or cream,
Has the wild berry plucked in June
Beside the trickling stream.

Robert Graves

Red currant

Gooseberry

Black currant

Raspberry

Strawberry

Cherry

Animal babies

Little Lamb,
Here I am;
Come and lick
My white neck;
Let me pull
Your soft wool;
Let me kiss
Your soft face:
Merrily, Merrily,
*   we welcome in*
*   the Year.*

William Blake

The fields grow full of lambs in the spring; this is the season of birth for many animals. At first, baby mammals feed on their mother's milk and spend much of the day asleep. Some animals are independent very young. Others stay with their mothers for some time after they are *weaned* (when they stop drinking their mothers' milk). Animal mothers carry their children in the womb for differing lengths of time before they are born. Some animals are born singly, others in litters.

Rabbit
pregnancy: 1 month
7-8 rabbits
adult at 1 month

Dog
pregnancy: 9 weeks
2-7 puppies
adult at 1 year

Cat
pregnancy: 8 weeks
3-6 kittens
adult at 1 year

84

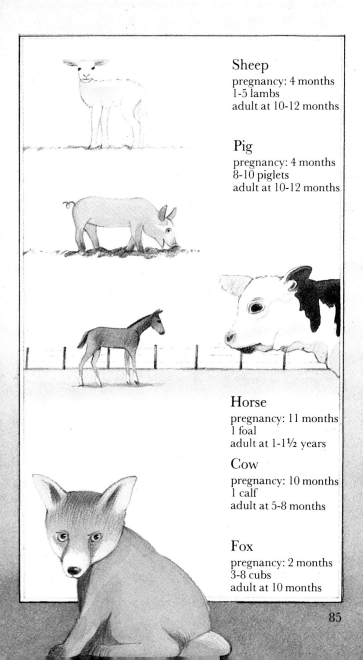

Sheep
pregnancy: 4 months
1-5 lambs
adult at 10-12 months

Pig
pregnancy: 4 months
8-10 piglets
adult at 10-12 months

Horse
pregnancy: 11 months
1 foal
adult at 1-1½ years

Cow
pregnancy: 10 months
1 calf
adult at 5-8 months

Fox
pregnancy: 2 months
3-8 cubs
adult at 10 months

Haymaking

*Green grass is all
I hear
And grass is all
I see
When through tall
fields I wander
Swish-swishing to
the knee.*

James Reeves

Farmers grow grass as food for their animals. They dry it to make hay, which keeps through the winter.

Grass for haymaking is cut in May and June, as it comes into flower. If left to go to seed, most grasses become tough and do not make such good hay.

In the old days, grass was cut with a scythe, raked into rows, and stacked into haycocks to dry. Then the hay was tossed into a cart with a pitchfork, to be taken to the farm-yard and built into a haystack. Nowadays machines cut, collect and pack the hay.

All the sun long it was running,
it was lovely,
The hay fields high as the house,
the tunes from the chimney it was air
And playing, lovely and watery
And fire green as grass.

Dylan Thomas

A spring dictionary

Annunciation
25 March is the feast of the Annunciation, at which an angel appeared to the Virgin Mary and told her that she was to be the mother of Jesus.

Antennae
Insects do not have noses like we do; they can smell, as well as feel and taste, with their antennae. Some insects taste with their feet; bees know if a flower is sweet as soon as they land on it.

Abrasion
Some birds get their spring plumage not by moulting, but by abrasion, rubbing the duller feathers away over the winter months to appear at their brightest and best in the spring. Blue tits and great tits do this.

Bees
Bees are very sensitive to changes in air pressure, and so make good weather forecasters. If they stay in their hives, rain is on the way.

Cuckoo
In April
Come he will.
In May
He sings all day.
In June
He changes tune.
In July
He prepares to fly.
In August
Go he must.

Ducks
The mother duck lays 9-11 eggs in spring. Shortly after hatching, ducklings can swim and eat water-weed.

Easter
The Anglo-Saxon goddess of spring was called Eostra. It is probably from her that the Christian feast of Easter got its name.

Fish

In May, at the bottom of the pond, the male stickleback builds a nest out of water-weed. Then he dances before his chosen female, hoping that she will enter his nest to lay her eggs. Salmon leave the sea in spring and swim up streams. They go back to lay their eggs in the rivers where they themselves were born.

St George

23 April is the feast of St George, the patron saint of England. He lived in the third or fourth century. Legend says that he rescued a princess from a dragon that was laying waste Libya.

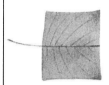

Hare

'Mad as a March hare': in the mating season hares behave strangely. They box with each other and drum on the ground with their paws.

Holi

In India people celebrate Holi, a spring festival lasting 5 days.

Insects

Creatures that look
Like pips and seeds
Sow themselves
* in the places*
No one else needs.
                Stanley Cook

Jay

In early spring, jays hold gatherings in which they chase each other, slowly flapping their wings. When courting, the male spreads out his tail and wings, which are edged with blue feathers. The jay's normally harsh cry grows quieter in the nesting season. The jay is a clever mimic of other birds, and can make itself sound just like a buzzard or a tawny owl to frighten other birds away.

June

June is named after Juno, the Roman goddess of love and fertility. The Romans used to believe that the month of June was the luckiest month in which to get married or engaged.

Kingfisher

The kingfisher has a beautiful blue-green back and chestnut breast. You can see it by streams and rivers through the spring and summer months. It sits quite still on a perch by water, then dives down when it spots a fish or insect. The male courts the female with an offering of food; if she accepts his fish, she will accept him as a mate too. Male and female together dig a hole in the bank for their nest. Kingfishers' nests are often full of rotting fishbones and can be smelly.

Lent

Lent is an old English word for spring – *lencten* meant 'to lengthen', referring to the lengthening day.

Maundy Thursday

The Thursday before Easter is known as Maundy or Holy Thursday. This is the feast of Christ's Last Supper with his apostles, when he gave them the commandment to love one another. 'Maundy' probably comes from the Latin word *mandatum*, meaning commandment. For many centuries monarchs, and the Pope and his bishops, would wash the feet of a number of poor people on Maundy Thursday, as a sign of humility and charity. Nowadays the English monarch gives out 'Maundy money'. As many men and women as there are years to the monarch's age receive bags of silver pennies – one penny for each year of the monarch's life.

Migration

Many birds migrate back to Europe in spring. Swallows, like cuckoos, leave Africa in March. They feed on insects and come to Europe when there are plenty for them to eat. Then, at the end of summer, they fly back to Africa.

Nectar

Flowers do not make nectar for themselves. They produce it to attract the insects which pollinate them.

Oranges and lemons

Say the bells of St Clement's

goes the old nursery rhyme. On 31 March a service is held at the church of St Clement Dane by the Thames. At the service children are given presents of oranges and lemons.

Osprey

This beautiful bird of prey has been saved from extinction in the UK by careful protection, and can be seen in spring.

Passover

Jewish spring festival commemorating the escape of the Ancient Jews from Egypt, when Moses led them across the Red Sea on the start of their long march to the promised land of Israel.

Poppies

Bright red flowers living mainly in chalkland. Like many flowers, poppies are pollinated by bees. But bees are colour-blind: to them a poppy is a white flower with a black centre. Because of their blood-red colour, and because they grow on the chalklands where many of the First World War battles were fought, poppies have become a symbol for all the soldiers killed in war.

Primrose

One of the very first wild flowers to bloom in springtime. Its name means 'first rose'.

Queen of May

In the old days, as part of the festivities for 1 May, a girl was crowned Queen of May.

Rainbow

Purple, yellow, red and green, The king cannot reach it, nor yet the queen; Nor can old Noll, whose power's so great; Tell me this riddle while I count eight.

Sheep shearing

You may shear your sheep When the elder blossoms peep.

Sheep are sheared soon after lambing time. Shearing used to be done using hand-clippers, but now machine-clippers are used, which go much faster. In Australia and New Zealand they have sheep-shearing competitions, to see how many sheep a man can shear in an hour.

Toad

It is not always the mother toad which rears the babies. The male *midwife toad* hatches eggs laid by the female, carrying them on his back.

Umbrella

*The rain it raineth
    on the just
And also on the
    unjust fella.
But chiefly on the
    just, because
The unjust steals
    the just's
    umbrella.*
        Lord Bowen

Violets

*Such a starved
    bank of moss
Till, that May morn,
Blue ran the
    flash across —
Violets were born.*
        Robert Browning

There are two kinds of violets, the scented 'sweet violet' and the scentless 'dog violet'. In olden days they used to make sweets out of violets, crystallizing the petals in sugar.

Voles

Voles live underground during the winter, eating roots. In spring they come out and feast on the buds and shoots.

Xylem

The xylem is the part of the trunk and branches of a tree through which water flows, rising from the roots to feed the buds and leaves.

Year

Our year is divided into 4 seasons. The Ancient Egyptians had 3 seasons: flood-time, seed-time and harvest-time. Their year began with the flooding of the Nile.

Zephyr

A poetical name for the gentle west wind that blows in spring.

Biographies

Georges Lemoine lives as much as he can in the country, in the heart of Normandy. An outstanding and well-known French watercolourist, exhibiting regularly in Paris art galleries, he started his career as a typographer and book designer, and still maintains his interest in those fields. He has worked in France as an illustrator for some of the most prominent authors of fiction, as well as illustrating innumerable book covers. *Spring* is his second information book; a few years ago he illustrated a lovely guide to trees.

Spring has won the French 'Loisirs-Jeunes' prize: the most important children's book prize in France.

Laurence Ottenheimer taught history and geography for a few years before working in publishing, where she specializes in activity and information books for young children.

Alex Campbell studied English literature at Oxford. Now the mother of two young children, she enjoys working on children's books while they are at school. In her work on the four *Discoverers* Season books, she has taken particular pleasure in choosing the poems.

Acknowledgements

The editor and publisher wish to thank the following for permission to use copyright material:

The Author for *I want an egg for Easter* by Irene F. Pawsey; the Author for *Wild Strawberries* from Poems 1914-1926 by Robert Graves; the Author for *So here we are in April* by Ted Robinson; the Author's Estate for *A Blackbird Suddenly* by Joseph Auslander; A. & C. Black for *The Speckled Frogs* by L.B. Scott © Bowmar 1954; Constable & Co. Ltd. for *The Apple Tree* from Collected Poems by Oliver St.John Gogarty; J.M. Dent and Sons for *Fern Hill* from Collected Poems by Dylan Thomas; André Deutsch Ltd. for *Tip-top tip-top* from You Can't Catch Me by Michael Rosen; Gerald Duckworth & Co. for *The Frog* from Cautionary Verses by Hilaire Belloc; Faber and Faber Ltd. for *New Hampshire* from Collected Poems by T.S. Eliot, and for *Spring Nature Notes 2* from Season Songs by Ted Hughes, and for *Trees* from High Windows by Philip Larkin; Granada Publishing Ltd. and the Liveright Publishing Corp. for *Spring is like a perhaps hand* from The Complete Poems by e.e. cummings; Hamish Hamilton Ltd. for *Spell of Creation* from Collected Poems by Kathleen Raine; William Heinemann Ltd. for *Green Grass* and *The moon is up* from Complete Poems for Children by James Reeves; Michael Joseph Ltd. for *To any garden* from Silver-sand and Snow by Eleanor Farjeon; The Literary Trustees of Walter de la Mare and The Society of Authors as their representative for *The Bees' Song* and for *The Fly* from Collected Rhymes and Verses by Walter de la Mare; Little, Brown & Co. for *The Ant* from I'm a Stranger Here Myself by Ogden Nash, and for *Listen, buds* by Ogden Nash; Herbert Nicholson as the literary executor for *A Hot Day* by A.S.J. Tessimond; Rinehart & Co., Inc. for *Was worm* from A Cage of Spines by May Swenson; Martin Secker and Warburg Ltd. for *Song* from Complete Poems by Andrew Young; Sidgwick & Jackson Ltd. for *A field for palms* and *Loveliest of trees* from A Shropshire Lad by A.E. Housman; The Society of Authors on behalf of the copyright owner, Mrs. Iris Wise, for *The Buds* from Collected Poems by James Stephens.